# THE GREAT BOOK OF
# OLYMPIC
# GAMES

WSKids
WHITE STAR KIDS

# THE GREAT BOOK OF
# OLYMPIC GAMES

TEXT BY
**VERUSKA MOTTA**

ILLUSTRATIONS BY
**LUCA POLI**

# CONTENTS

**EVERY FOUR YEARS, BILLIONS OF PEOPLE GATHER IN FRONT OF THEIR TV OR ASSEMBLE IN SQUARES IN FRONT OF A SCREEN, HOLDING THEIR BREATH. SOMETIMES THEY CRY, SOMETIMES THEY LAUGH, AND SOMETIMES THEY JUMP FROM THEIR SEATS, HUGGING ONE ANOTHER.**

*What are they watching that is so moving? What is this strange, crazy euphoria that affects everyone? And how can it reach every corner of the world?*

### THE MYSTERY IS SOLVED: THE OLYMPIC GAMES!

Every athlete dreams of this moment, training rigorously year after year for the most important competition of all. Getting to the Games is very difficult: only the best champions of each country manage to enter them.

**BUT . . . WHAT DOES IT MEAN TO BE A CHAMPION?**

Some of the athletes challenge gravity through exceptionally high (or extremely long) jumps, others run so fast that they don't even seem to touch the ground, and others swim so well as to rival and beat fish and mermaids! However, this is not enough.

**OLYMPIC CHAMPIONS HAVE SOMETHING SPECIAL.**

**They have big hearts and the courage to overcome seemingly impossible hurdles, managing to win. But they also have the humanity to relinquish first place in support of a struggling fellow athlete.**

The Olympic Games are a two-week journey that can make dreams come true, either through some very popular sports (a few of which you may have tried yourself at least once) or others that are quite unusual yet fascinating. There are competitions that last only for a few seconds, with everybody holding their breath anticipating the result, and there are some that are very long, lasting many hours, where points are scored one by one.

**THE GAMES ARE THE SUDDEN RUSH OF EMOTION AND THE TEARS POURED OVER A FLAG.**

**SO, ARE YOU READY?**

**LET'S DISCOVER THE OLYMPIC GAMES TOGETHER!**

# THE ORIGINS OF THE OLYMPIC GAMES

THE STREETS OF OLYMPIA HAVE BEEN FILLING UP WITH PEOPLE SINCE THE EARLY HOURS OF THE MORNING. PEOPLE HAVE COME HERE TO SELL THEIR GOODS, TO BET ON A CHAMPION'S VICTORY, OR TO SIMPLY CHEER WITH HAPPINESS AT THE FINISHING LINE. THE WHOLE CITY IS IN A FRENZY. AFTER ALL, THIS IS AN IMPORTANT OCCASION: THE OLYMPIC GAMES ARE CELEBRATING THEIR 25TH ANNIVERSARY.

A century has already passed since the first Games, and there is a surprise this year: the program includes the **QUADRIGA**, a race between **chariots drawn by four horses.** The luckiest people have seen the animals enter the stables near the arena: mighty and powerful creatures, with shiny coats, pawing the ground impatiently. Their trainers hold them back by the reins . . .

This was happening in **680 BC**. However, those emotions, that electricity in the air and the waiting for each competition, feel so similar to what happens nowadays.

Every Olympic Games are a concentration of truly incredible and passionate stories, of commitment and strokes of luck (or bad luck!), of dedication and endless dreams that all converge into that long-awaited finish line.

Why was it decided to organize this competition?

Why did the athletes speak only Greek?

**AND WERE THOSE ANCIENT SPORTS THE SAME AS THE MODERN ONES?**

# TWO ORIGINS: MYTH VS. HISTORY

The ancient Greeks believed that the gods of Olympus controlled the lives of humans (even by interfering with them). The Olympic Games couldn't be an exception then . . .

One of the origin legends says that the founder of the Olympic Games was the heroic **HERACLES**, also known as **HERCULES**, a demigod son of a woman and Zeus, the father of all gods. Heracles had to face harsh **battles** against monsters and legendary creatures in the famous **TWELVE LABORS** (and they were aptly named).

But that's not all. After winning all of his challenges, he decided to organize a running competition with his brothers. **He wasn't lazy at all, was he?**

We know for sure that the very first Olympic Games were held in **776 BC** in the city of Olympia, near a big temple dedicated to Zeus. And even if the idea of a competition between demigods (half-god and half-human) is more exciting, it is most likely that the **OLYMPICS** were born out of an agreement between two Greek kings. Tired of being at war with each other, they wanted to celebrate peace and to thank Zeus by organizing a big sporting event.

**MUCH BETTER TO COMPETE ON A GAME FIELD THAN IN A BATTLEFIELD!**

# WIN IN PEACE

Unfortunately, in ancient times, wars were a common occurrence. But the governments that organized the Olympic Games agreed to respect the Ekecheiria (the Olympic Truce), which was basically a period of cessation of hostilities.

That is why it was thought for a long time that during the **Games**, every soldier in every part of Greece would put his weapon down. In actual fact, the athletes, the coaches, the audience, and the merchants who traveled to Olympia were very safe, even on their way there, whereas **everyone else had to keep watching their back!**

## Why?

The Truce was also a (temporary) period when kings and politicians would meet to discuss agreements and create alliances. And because they would do it in **OLYMPIA**, invasions and conflicts in other territories would continue.

Try to imagine what a **relief** it must have been: every four years, between the end of July and the beginning of August, thousands of people could go and attend the competitions without having to worry about "accidents" along the way.

The Games were taken very seriously by soldiers—whoever dared to break the Ekecheiria was punished by the gods. The athletes also took the Games very seriously and had only one thought in their mind: **first place**!

Yes, while today we give a prize for second and third place, **at that time only the winner would receive an award.**

# WHAT DID YOU SAY IT'S CALLED?

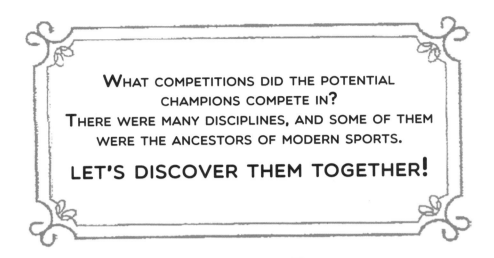

WHAT COMPETITIONS DID THE POTENTIAL CHAMPIONS COMPETE IN? THERE WERE MANY DISCIPLINES, AND SOME OF THEM WERE THE ANCESTORS OF MODERN SPORTS.

**LET'S DISCOVER THEM TOGETHER!**

### RUNNING

First of all was **RUNNING**, in which the fastest athletes in Greece had to cover at least one "stadion." No, it had nothing to do with football matches—a "stadion" was an ancient unit of measure (1 stadion corresponded to approximately 193 yards [177 m]—and the hardest race was 24 stadions long, which was 2.6 miles [4.2 km]).

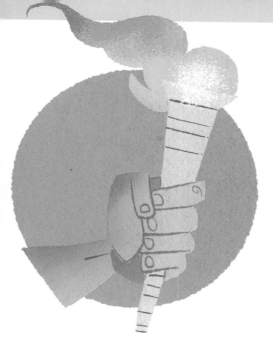

## THE LAMPADEDROMIA

Then there was the **LAMPADEDROMIA**, which was the first version of the relay race. Each team consisted of 40 members, each of whom had to run 82 feet (25 m) while holding a flaming torch aloft! It might seem hard to believe, but it did work like that! Today, there are only 4 sprinters, and they pass a "simple" baton. Definitely safer but less spectacular.

## THE HOPLITODROMOS

And what about a race where the athletes carried over 40 pounds (20 kg) of iron and animal skins on their shoulders (also running barefoot)? The **HOPLITODROMOS** was a tough competition: only the strongest and best trained athletes could endure it.

These super athletes would run with their helmet on their head while wearing full war gear. Although this game no longer exists in the modern Olympics, it is still part of soldiers' training.

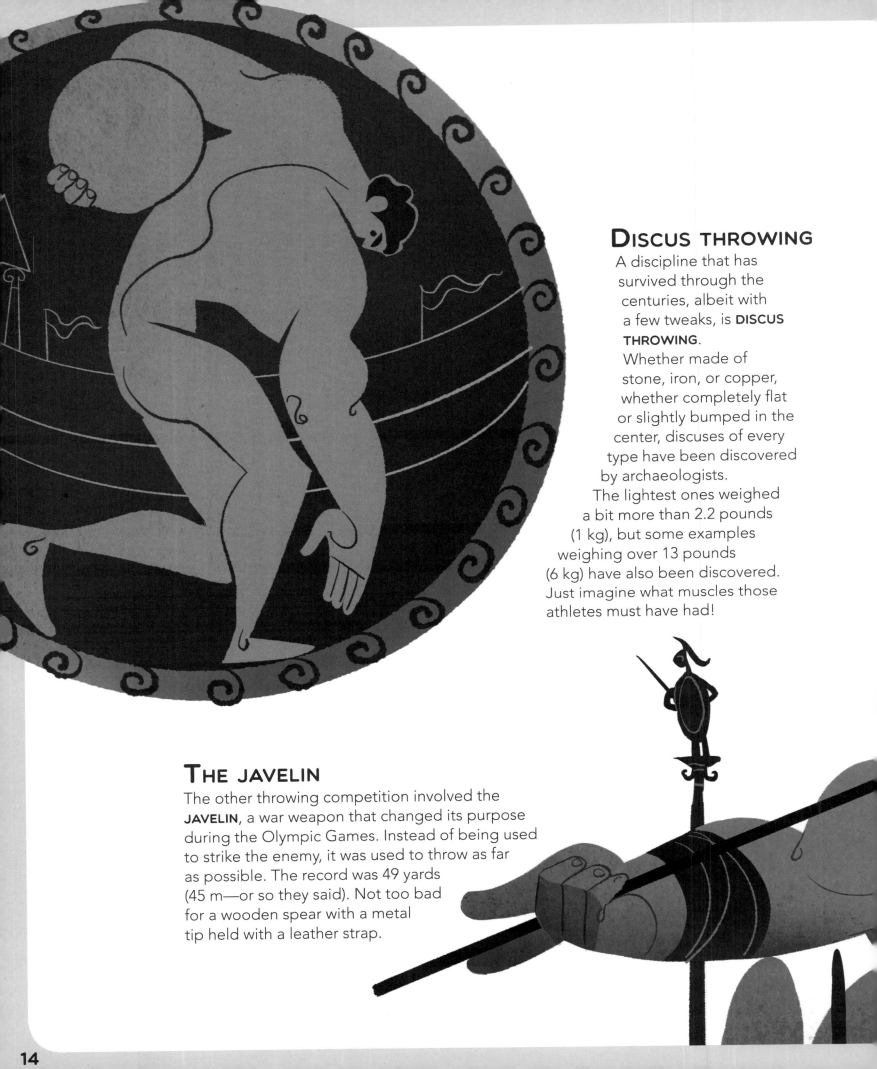

## DISCUS THROWING

A discipline that has survived through the centuries, albeit with a few tweaks, is **DISCUS THROWING**.

Whether made of stone, iron, or copper, whether completely flat or slightly bumped in the center, discuses of every type have been discovered by archaeologists.

The lightest ones weighed a bit more than 2.2 pounds (1 kg), but some examples weighing over 13 pounds (6 kg) have also been discovered. Just imagine what muscles those athletes must have had!

## THE JAVELIN

The other throwing competition involved the **JAVELIN**, a war weapon that changed its purpose during the Olympic Games. Instead of being used to strike the enemy, it was used to throw as far as possible. The record was 49 yards (45 m—or so they said). Not too bad for a wooden spear with a metal tip held with a leather strap.

## THE LONG JUMP

There were also athletes who competed by throwing themselves. Exactly! Those performing the **LONG JUMP** had to leap as far as possible in a single action. This wouldn't have been very different from the modern discipline if it hadn't been for the fact that the ancient Greek athletes had to jump while holding two 8.8 pound (4 kg) weights!

**A PUNISHMENT?** Apparently not, as they were sure that in this way, they could improve the distance they could reach (funny, isn't it? Of course, we know today that this was not true).

# HAND-TO-HAND COMBAT!

Among the audience's favorite competitions, hand-to-hand combat had a special place.

Along with **WRESTLING**, which entailed spectacular moves, they had **BOXING**, in a form even more violent than the modern one. Athletes wouldn't wear any protection on their hands or on their face, and the blows were allowed even when the opponent was on the ground. It was a savage sport that was very much appreciated even by poets and intellectuals.

PLATO IN PARTICULAR REALLY ENJOYED PRACTICING IT. (LUCKILY, HE HAD MUCH MORE SUCCESS WITH PHILOSOPHY!)

## The pankration

The most extreme discipline, though, was an ancient form of modern wrestling with less rules and many, many more broken bones. It was the **PANKRATION**, a type of fighting where (almost) everything was allowed: punching, hitting with the knees and elbows, head-butting. Only gouging out the opponent's eyes was prohibited! The winner was the one who didn't surrender!

## The quadriga

What was the most anticipated race? Without a doubt, the **QUADRIGA:** a breathtaking race with war chariots, each one drawn by four horses. It was spectacular, yet very dangerous. The opponents would crash against one another, topple over, and sometimes end up off the track and hitting the spectators!

# THE OLYMPIC PROGRAM

THE FIRST OLYMPIC GAMES LASTED ONE DAY, AND THE ONLY COMPETITION WAS THE RUNNING ONE. THEY WERE LIGHTNING-FAST GAMES!

THEN OTHER SPORTS PROGRESSIVELY ENTERED AS PART OF THE PROGRAM, THEREBY INCREASING THE DURATION OF THE GAMES.

HERE ARE THE DIFFERENT STAGES:

Running (1 stadion)

Wrestling and pentathlon (the most difficult competition: athletes had to run for 1 stadion, make a long jump, throw the discus, throw the javelin, and to finish off, wrestle)

Boxing

**720 BC**

**688 BC**

**776 BC**

**708 BC**

**680 BC**

Long running
(7 to 24
stadions)

Quadriga

Boxing for the
younger ones (oh yes,
ancient Greeks really
loved fighting!)

Running (1 stadion)
and wrestling for the
younger ones

Pankration for
the younger ones
(incredible but true!)

**648 BC**

**628 BC**

**396 BC**

**632 BC**

**616 BC**

**200 BC**

Pankration and
horse race

Pentathlon for the
younger ones (it was
the only occasion it was
included—maybe it
was too much for them)

Competitions
for heralds (high
officials) and for
trumpeters (even those
who wrote or played
well deserved
a prize!)

# RITUALS AND EMOTIONS

THE TWELVE JUDGES AND THE ATHLETES ARE LINED UP IN FRONT OF THE TEMPLE.
THE EMOTION MAKES THEIR HEARTS BEAT FAST: IT IS TIME TO MAKE THE OATH TO ZEUS.

HERE IS THE SALPINX PLAYING!
THE SOUND OF THIS BRONZE TRUMPET
FILLS UP THE STREETS OF OLYMPIA.
LET THE GAMES BEGIN!

The opening ceremony was a
very important moment. The
eyes of thousands of people
were fixed on the athletes, and
everybody shared the same
thought: **Who will wear the
crown of olive branches, the
symbol of the winner?**

The competitions were undoubtedly the heart of the Olympic Games, but there were also other—equally important—**RITUALS** to perform in order to not upset the gods.

**For example, every activity was suspended on the third day to thank Zeus.**

**How?** A hundred oxen were sacrificed (what a terrible thing!) during a ceremony called **hecatomb**, a word that is still used today to indicate a disastrous event.

How can we know so much about rituals and sports that have been gone for **centuries**? The credit all goes . . . to **POTTERY**!

The Olympic Games were one of the favorite subjects of the artists of that time, who enjoyed painting the athletes on any type of vessel.

### ATHENIANS

Elegant and sophisticated, but also a bit vain.

### CITIZENS OF OLYMPIA

The luckiest ones, as they played at home!

### SPARTANS

Expert warriors, always ready to fight their opponents.

### CRETANS

Their rich red tunics would stand out from the crowd.

# ANCIENT GREECE

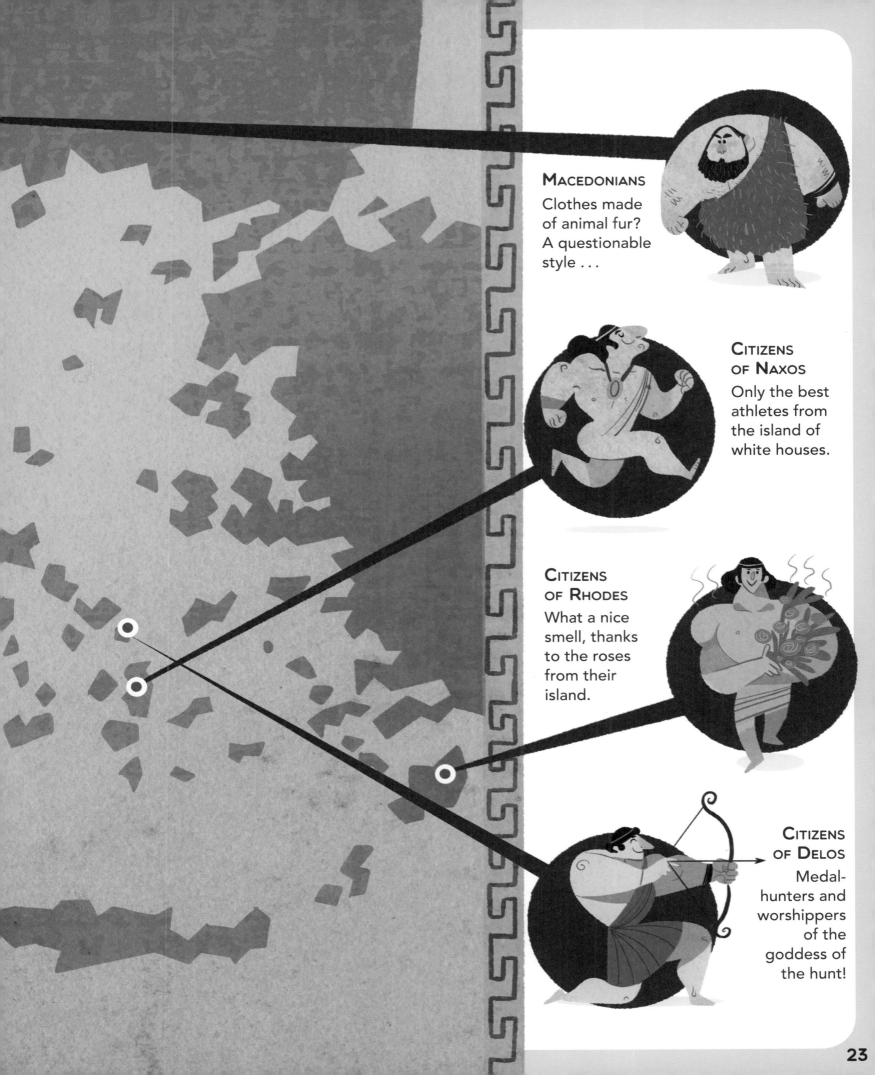

**MACEDONIANS**
Clothes made of animal fur? A questionable style . . .

**CITIZENS OF NAXOS**
Only the best athletes from the island of white houses.

**CITIZENS OF RHODES**
What a nice smell, thanks to the roses from their island.

**CITIZENS OF DELOS**
Medal-hunters and worshippers of the goddess of the hunt!

# ATHLETES: HEROES OR GODS?

TODAY, THE OLYMPIC GAMES ATTRACT ATHLETES FROM ALL OVER THE WORLD, BUT IN THE BEGINNING, THE GAMES WERE ONLY FOR A FEW SELECT ONES. ONLY THE GREEKS (I.E., ONLY THOSE BORN TO PARENTS WHO WERE BOTH GREEK) COULD PARTICIPATE.

The contestants had to show up in Olympia a month before the start of the Games. No excuses were accepted. The late ones were punished either with a fine or by being disqualified!

**WHAT ABOUT THOSE WHO CHANGED THEIR MINDS?** During the "training bootcamp" (which was an intensive training period lasting 10 months), it was possible to step back, preserving one's dignity. Doing the same while the Games were ongoing simply meant becoming the laughingstock of all of Greece. **No, it was not worth it.** After all, if an athlete was already there, they may as well try their best to win and have a chance to be remembered forever, like an **IMMORTAL CREATURE**!

# THE LOOK OF AN ATHLETE

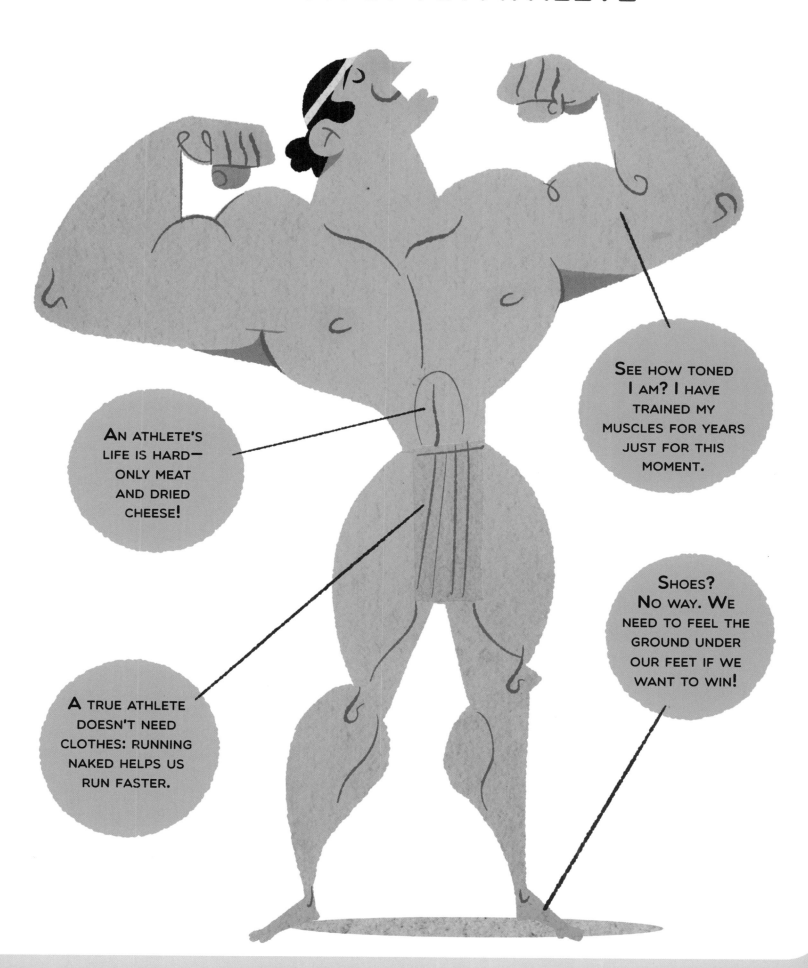

# CHAMPIONS OF THE PAST

### LEONIDAS OF RHODES

"He was as fast as a god." Not too bad a description for a runner. Leonidas of Rhodes was not just a special athlete, he was also unique: 2,000 years had to pass before someone else could break his records! He was the absolute champion of 4 Olympic Games, from 164 to 152 BC. His 16 years of success was not just in running but also in hoplitodromos (he was unbeatable even with 44 pounds—20 kg—of armor on).

THAT IS WHY PEOPLE WOULD LINE UP TO SEE HIM, AS IF HE WAS A MODERN ROCK STAR!

## NERO

We usually remember Nero as the emperor who set Rome on fire (at least that is what the legend says), but he was also an Olympic champion: in 67 AD, he won **5 disciplines**.

WITH A LITTLE HELP, THOUGH. He had the Games postponed for 2 years so that he could train, and then he participated in the 3 disciplines that had been created specifically for him.

BUT THAT'S NOT ALL. During the horse race, the other contestants had to slow down to let him win!

# OEBOTAS

Oebotas was the first athlete from Achaea (a historical region of Greece) to win the Olympics. However, his people ignored him. So much effort and not even a small celebration!

SO HE CURSED THEM, AND NO ACHAEAN ATHLETE WON ANYTHING FOR THE FOLLOWING 300 YEARS.

Never provoke an athlete's anger!

## MILO OF CROTON

The superhuman power of Milo of Croton was **legendary**. He was the strongest wrestler in Greece from a young age, and he won **7 OLYMPIC GAMES IN A ROW** (the first time when he had just turned 15).

But he was not just a sport champion. He also studied **philosophy** and fought like a lion. Nothing could really scare him. Once during an earthquake, he saved some people by substituting himself for a broken pillar. He basically held the weight of the whole roof so that everybody could escape!

## TIMASITEUS OF CROTON

In 516 BC, the young Timasiteus of Croton came face to face with his fellow citizen **MILO**.

How could he fight against his hero, the **idol** of all crowds who was worshipped like a god? **NO, IT WAS NOT POSSIBLE!** So, he refused—a noble gesture that (for once) gained the second-place winner eternal glory.

## ERODORUS

The true **MAN OF RECORDS** was without a doubt Erodorus, who won **10 CONSECUTIVE OLYMPIC GAMES** (from 328 BC to 292 BC).

He had a great lung capacity, but he didn't run. He had a strong physique, but not because of his muscles. **HIS SPECIALTY?** He was the best of the **trumpeters** (at that time, they had been competing in the Games for quite a while).

**AND HE WAS A CHAMPION EVEN AT THE TABLE BECAUSE HE WOULD EAT AND DRINK LIKE ONE!**

# STORIES OF EXTRAORDINARY WOMEN

RUNNERS, WRESTLERS, THROWERS—
ALL OF THEM WERE MEN. THE OLYMPIC
GAMES WERE EXCLUSIVE TO MEN
(WOMEN WERE FORBIDDEN EVEN
TO ATTEND THE GAMES).
INCREDIBLE, ISN'T IT?

HOWEVER, THERE WAS SOMEONE WHO HAD THE COURAGE TO BREAK SUCH UNFAIR RULES.

CALLIPATERA, who was the mother and coach of a young athlete, wore men's clothes to disguise herself in the crowd. After her son's victory, she jumped over the fences and ran to embrace him—**and she lost her tunic**!
It was a real **SCANDAL**. Fortunately, her family was one of Olympic champions and so she was soon forgiven. From that day, spectators were **required to undress** before taking their seats: they had to be easily recognizable!

# Cynisca of Sparta

Even more famous than Calliptera was Cynisca of Sparta, a finely skilled **horse trainer**. Just a few words from her, and horses would obey completely (incredible!). If only she could have had the chance to participate in the Games . . .

She came from a people of warriors, men and women who were raised to never surrender in the face of adversity. Why should SHE do so? She found a solution.
The racehorses had to be ridden by men, but the rules didn't say anything about **trainers**.
So she showed up at the hippodrome, leaving everybody speechless.

**No, it wasn't a joke: Cynisca won the race, and she was forever remembered for that.**

# STRANGE BUT TRUE!

## WONDERFUL!

The statue of Zeus would strike everybody entering the temple in Olympia and leave them speechless.
With its **42 foot (13 m) height**, made of **gold** and **ivory** by **PHIDIAS** himself (who was the most famous sculptor in ancient Greece), it was so imposing that the head of the father of all gods almost touched the ceiling of the building.
It stayed there for over **800 years**, a wonder for every pilgrim.
UNFORTUNATELY, IT NO LONGER EXISTS (IT WAS DESTROYED BY A FIRE), BUT IT IS CONSIDERED ONE OF THE SEVEN WONDERS OF THE ANCIENT WORLD.

# BEWARE OF FALSE STARTS!

Each athlete had to make the oath of respecting the rules. **What happened to those who were trying to get around those rules?** Sometimes athletes would cheat by beginning the race before the official start to gain time over their opponents.

**The punishments were harsh for everyone!** In the best case, they would end up paying a high fine. But if the judges got really angry, it could end up with a **flogging**!

## RUNNER OR BAKER?

The first winner of the Olympic Games that we know of was the runner **Coroebus**.

Was he a famous athlete? A sportsman who had dedicated years to training? Not at all: **he was a baker!**

# TELL ME HOW MUCH OF A BEARD YOU HAVE AND I WILL TELL YOU WHERE TO COMPETE!

The twelve Olympic judges had the task of dividing the contestants into **young** and adult so they could compete in their respective categories.

HOWEVER, UNLIKE TODAY, THERE WERE NO IDENTIFICATION DOCUMENTS IN ANCIENT GREECE.

So how could they establish the athletes' age (and include them in the right group) without making any mistakes? SIMPLE. THEY JUST NEEDED TO . . . measure their beards! A rather approximate method for sure, but actually quite funny.

# HOW MANY OLYMPIC GAMES ARE YOU?

Thousands of years ago, each city had its own **CALENDAR**. Imagine how confusing it must have been to arrange appointments!

However, from **776 BC** on, it became possible to measure time by using the Olympic Games as a reference. After all, everybody knew that **one Olympic Games corresponded to 4 years**. For example, if we had asked a child how old they were, they could have responded: "I'm two Olympics old" (i.e., 8 years old).

# THAT TIME WHEN A DEAD MAN WON!

**PANKRATION** was a dangerous sport, so much so that sometimes athletes lost their lives (yes, it would happen).

At that time, nobody would get too upset about that, except when a certain **ARRHICHION OF PHIGALIA** competed and something incredible happened to him. Suffocated by his opponent, before dying, he managed to deliver a final strike to his opponent's knee, so hard that in the end it was the opponent who was the first to give in.

**THE GAME WAS THEREFORE WON BY A DEAD MAN!**

# AND IN THE END ...

OVER 1,000 CONSECUTIVE YEARS OF OLYMPIC GAMES AND TRUCES—WHAT AN EXTRAORDINARY STORY! THE BEST ATHLETES FACED ONE ANOTHER, COMPETED IN EXTREMELY HARD RACES, HONORED ZEUS, AND ENTERED HISTORY (THANKS TO THE WORKS OF HISTORIANS, ARTISTS, AND POETS) FOR 292 CONSECUTIVE GAMES.

BUT IN 393 AD, THE GREAT ADVENTURE OF THE ANCIENT GAMES STOPPED.

Greece lost its prestige. The **Romans** conquered the whole of the **Mediterranean,** and people put mythology and the GODS OF OLYMPUS to one side. Emperor **THEODOSIUS** decided to **cancel the Olympic Games**: nobody was interested in them anymore.

And nobody had the inspiration to re-organize this type of competition for ALMOST **1,500 YEARS**.

In this period, people just thought about fighting one another in **wars** to obtain more **power** or more **territories** (sometimes both).

However, there had to be a peaceful way to channel the rivalry between nations, to fight through sport, rather than on the battleground.
AND IN **1894**, BARON PIERRE DE COUBERTIN HAD AN IDEA . . . .

# A MAN WITH A GREAT IDEA

PARIS-BORN PIERRE (THE NOBLEMAN WHO HAD THE INSPIRATION) REALLY LIKED SPORTS AND COULDN'T GET HIS HEAD AROUND THE FACT THAT PEOPLE WOULD PREFER FIGHTING INSTEAD OF RUNNING, JUMPING, OR THROWING A BALL. IN ACTUAL FACT, EVEN DURING TIMES OF PEACE, VERY FEW PEOPLE USED TO ENJOY EXERCISE (EVEN CHILDREN WERE ALWAYS AT HOME OR AT SCHOOL).

Why wouldn't everyone appreciate the advantages physical exercise brought to the body and to the mind?

In order to become athletes (or even simply to practice a sport), it is necessary to **learn how to concentrate** to reach a certain goal, make sacrifices, and respect the opponents and the rules. Pierre knew that very well. That's way he couldn't help but think that sport had the power to change the world. **But how?**

There was an event that had managed to unite populations (at least some of them) in the past, **so why not replicate it?**
In **1894**, during a **special congress in Paris**, Pierre proposed to organize the new **International Olympic Games.**

The news went around the world and was met with great enthusiasm. In a very short time, the **IOC** (International Olympic Committee) was born, establishing the Games again **every 4 years** but changing the host nation each time.
**The spirit of the Games had to be carried to every country!**

The first modern Olympic Games were held in **1896**.
Where? It could only have been one location:
**Greece, where everything had started.**

# EXISTING SPORTS AND SPORTS THAT HAVE DISAPPEARED

A lot has changed since the first modern Olympic Games. For example, **285 athletes** from **14 countries** took part in 1896, whereas we have reached almost **11,000 athletes** from over **200 countries**! Step by step, Pierre's dream has come true: THE GAMES HAVE TRULY BECOME INTERNATIONAL. Even the number of sports has increased.

There were 9 at the beginning, and look how many there are now:

- Athletics
- Badminton
- Soccer
- Canoeing/Kayaking
- Rowing
- Cycling
- Equestrianism
- Gymnastics (artistic, rhythmic, and acrobatic)
- Golf
- Polo
- Judo
- Wrestling
- Basketball
- Handball
- Volleyball and beach volleyball
- Pentathlon
- Boxing
- Rugby sevens
- Fencing
- Weightlifting
- Water sports (swimming, synchronized swimming, water polo, diving)
- Taekwondo
- Tennis
- Table tennis
- Shooting
- Archery
- Triathlon
- Sailing

## AND STARTING FROM TOKYO WE ALSO HAVE:

- Climbing
- Baseball/Softball
- Karate
- Skateboarding
- Surfing

## SPORTS THAT HAVE DISAPPEARED

There were also some **curious** disciplines that were dropped at some point, including **solo synchronized swimming** (who was the athlete supposed to synchronize themself with?), **hot-air balloon**, **tandem cycling** (a bicycle for two people), **tug-of-war,** and **obstacle race . . . in the water!**

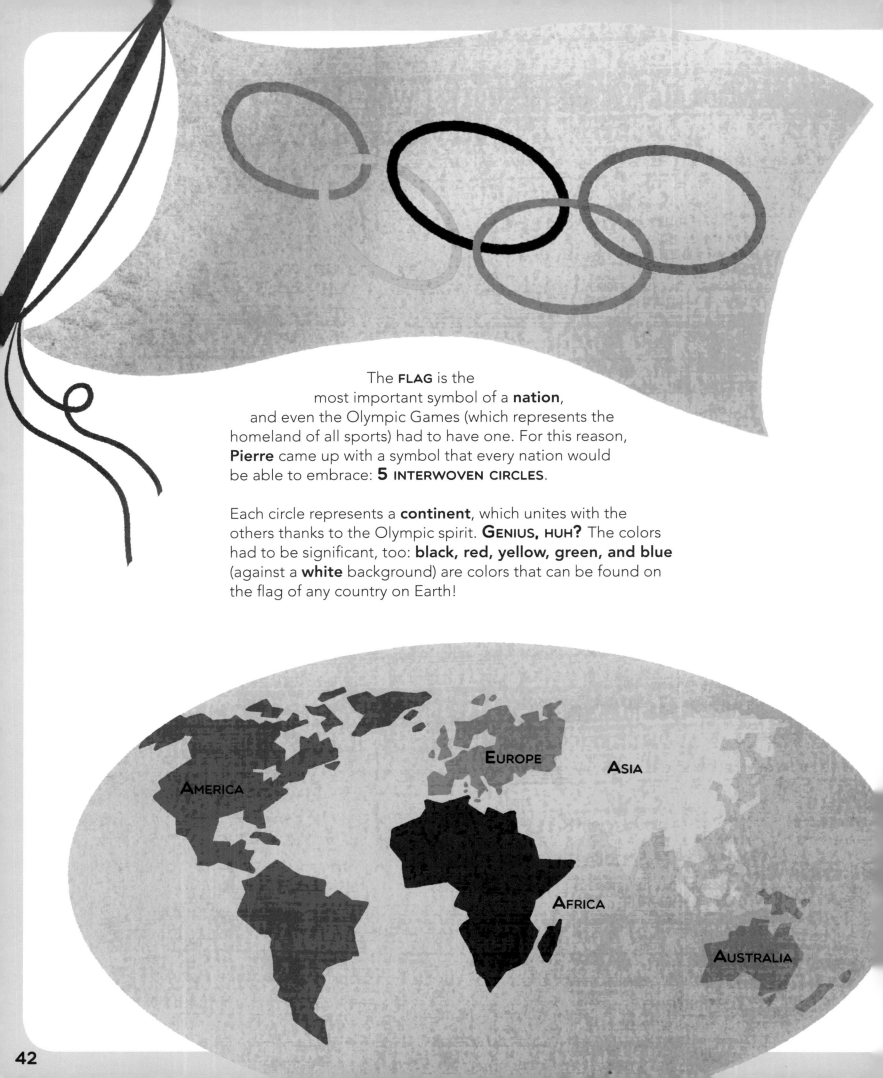

The **FLAG** is the
most important symbol of a **nation**,
and even the Olympic Games (which represents the
homeland of all sports) had to have one. For this reason,
**Pierre** came up with a symbol that every nation would
be able to embrace: **5 INTERWOVEN CIRCLES**.

Each circle represents a **continent**, which unites with the
others thanks to the Olympic spirit. **GENIUS, HUH?** The colors
had to be significant, too: **black, red, yellow, green, and blue**
(against a **white** background) are colors that can be found on
the flag of any country on Earth!

EUROPE

ASIA

AMERICA

AFRICA

AUSTRALIA

# WHAT MATTERS IS NOT THE WINNING BUT THE TAKING PART

Each team has its **MOTTO**, so they had to find one for the event that unites all sports (or at least most of them). Officially, it is *Citius! Altius! Fortius!* (Faster! Higher! Stronger!), but the one that you probably have heard more often is: **"What matters is not the winning but the taking part!"**

Many believe that these words came from Pierre, but actually he was inspired by a **bishop's speech**. In the end, it doesn't really matter where they came from. What's important is that they express the values upon which the Games were founded. **Acceptance, friendship, solidarity, and fair play** (as in fairness and respect toward the opponents) are the qualities that each Olympic athlete should live by.

# THE OLYMPIC TORCH

SINCE THE GAMES WERE FIRST ORGANIZED, THEIR SYMBOL HAS BEEN A TORCH. NOWADAYS, THE FAMOUS OLYMPIC TORCH IS LIT DURING A SYMBOLIC ANCIENT RITUAL THAT BEGINS IN OLYMPIA.

A group of **WOMEN**, dressed as Greek priestesses, light the torch using the heat generated by the sun's rays hitting a parabolic mirror. From there, the torch is **CARRIED AROUND THE WORLD**, until it reaches the city where the Olympic Games are hosted.

**IT IS USUALLY CARRIED BY TORCHBEARERS ON FOOT.**

But recently, it has started traveling by different means: **AIRPLANES**, **CAMELS**, canoes—even **UNDERWATER** and in **SPACE**! It went into orbit three times between **1996** and **2014**, but it had to be put out (otherwise, it would have been a bit of a problem on a shuttle!).

# THE MASCOTS

Since 1972, the Olympic Games have always had their mascots (some kind of lucky charm). Some of them became so famous that they were turned into cartoon characters; others have been widely forgotten.

## WALDI
### (Munich 1972)

Waldi was the **FIRST** official mascot—a **DACHSHUND**! Very funny but not very athletic. What do you think?

## MISHA
### (Moscow 1980)

Misha was a sweet **BEAR** that conquered every child's (**AND EVERYBODY ELSE'S**) heart!

## IZZY
### (Atlanta 1996)

Izzy was . . . well, even after decades nobody has understood what this big-eyed **CREATURE** is. **A MYSTERY**!

## MIRAITOWA AND SOMEITY
### (Tokyo 2020)

Miraitowa and Someity are **COLORFUL** and **FUNNY**, and they seem to have come straight out of a cartoon (they were chosen by **children in Japanese schools!**).

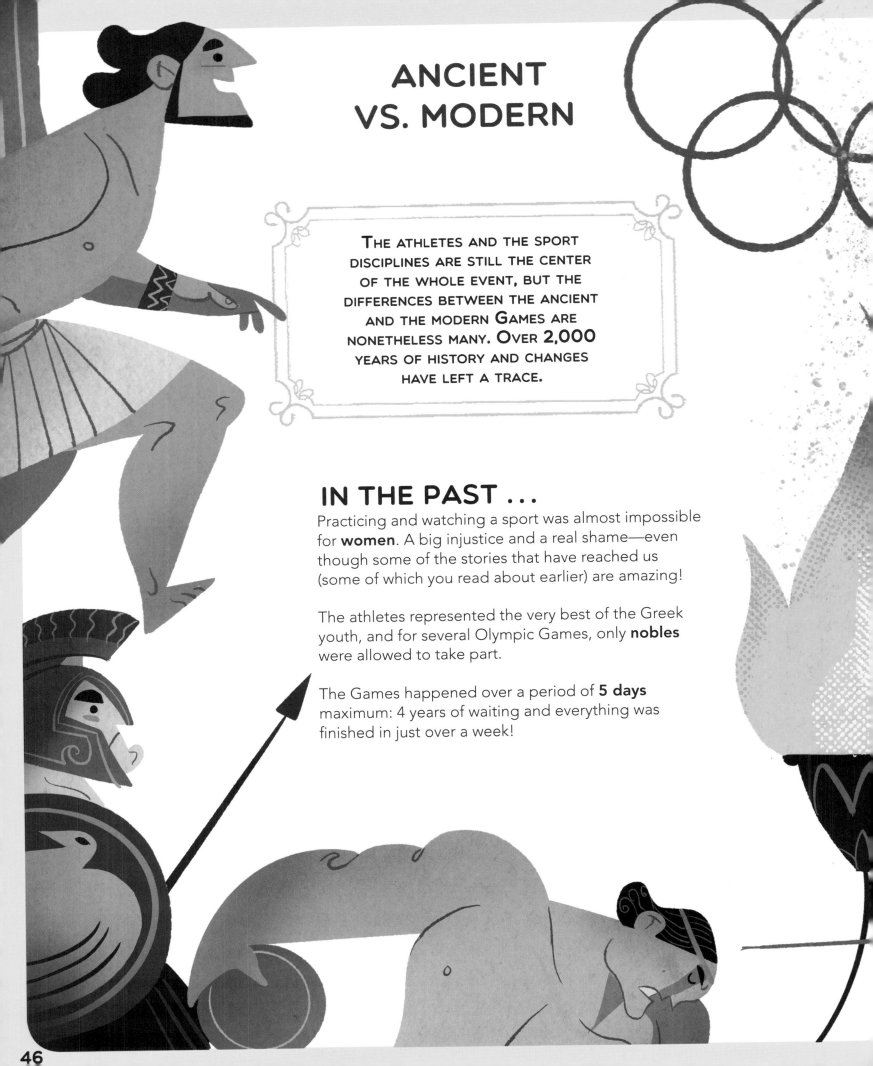

# ANCIENT VS. MODERN

The athletes and the sport disciplines are still the center of the whole event, but the differences between the ancient and the modern Games are nonetheless many. Over 2,000 years of history and changes have left a trace.

## IN THE PAST ...

Practicing and watching a sport was almost impossible for **women**. A big injustice and a real shame—even though some of the stories that have reached us (some of which you read about earlier) are amazing!

The athletes represented the very best of the Greek youth, and for several Olympic Games, only **nobles** were allowed to take part.

The Games happened over a period of **5 days** maximum: 4 years of waiting and everything was finished in just over a week!

## ... AND TODAY

Women were excluded from the first modern Olympic Games. Pierre was of the idea that female sport wasn't that interesting (even the best ones are wrong sometimes!).

However, starting in the following Games (**Paris 1900**), women started competing IN MORE AND MORE DISCIPLINES. Since **2012**, finally, THERE HAVEN'T BEEN ANY MORE EXCLUSIVELY MALE GAMES!

For over 90 years, the Olympic Games were restricted to amateurs, those who practiced sport as a passion (but not with continuity). From **1988**, even **professionals** (those who practice sport as their job) have been allowed to take part.

Today, the Games last about **14 days**. The record was reached in 1908 when they started in April and ended in June (A LOT OF WORK!).

# WHAT A RECORD!

Certainly, each Olympic Games have given us exceptional stories and breathtaking competitions. However, some athletes have reached such extraordinary heights that they have become part of history.

For instance, swimmer **Michael Phelps** won 28 medals (8 in the same Games), beating gymnast **Larisa Latynina**, who was in second place among the "super athletes," by 10 medals. There have also been talented athletes who stood out in more than one sport. For example, **Frank Kugler** triumphed in 3 different disciplines during the 1904 Saint Louis Olympic Games (wrestling, weightlifting, and tug-of-war).

Incredible, huh? Nobody has managed to break his record!

France, **Great Britain**, **Greece,** and **Switzerland** hold the RECORD FOR PARTICIPATING IN THE MOST Olympic Games.

**The United States** and **Soviet Union** (this was the name Russia and some neighboring countries used to have) have had the greatest number of **MEDALS**. Almost 3,000 for the USA—you would need a huge room to exhibit them all!

These records penalize the smaller countries, though (and those where sport is not practiced much) because they didn't take part in the first modern Games. And also, they have **fewer inhabitants** so they have fewer people to send to the Games!

Keeping the **population** in mind, the record goes to **FINLAND** (55.8 medals for every 1 million citizens).

**AND WHAT WAS THE MOST SUCCESSFUL OLYMPIC GAMES?** The one in **Atlanta**, with 8.3 million tickets sold!

# AGE DOESN'T MATTER!

### MARJORIE GESTRING

She was only 13 (and had a long journey from the USA to Berlin behind her) when she stepped onto the **9.8 foot (3 m) springboard**. A deep breath and then **jump**! The blonde girl from California became the youngest gold medalist in the history of the Games, thanks to a spectacular dive.

### OSCAR GOMER SWAHN

Sweden's Oscar Gomer Swahn simply didn't accept being old. When he was **64**, he won the gold medal in **shooting**, but that was not all. When he was **72**, he got the title as the oldest participant in the Olympics ... and a silver medal!

## SONJA HENIE

She was one of the greatest **figure skaters** ever. However, when competing in her first Olympic Games in 1924, she came in eighth. No podium then, but she got the medal for the **youngest attendant of the Games**—at that time, she hadn't turned **12!**

## WALTER RUDOLPH WALSH

**WHAT WAS THE CAKE WITH THE HIGHEST NUMBER OF CANDLES?** Well, undoubtedly that of Walter Rudolph Walsh. About to turn **107**, he was recognized as the world's oldest former Olympic athlete. He was also a famous **FBI** agent, who chased super-criminals such as **BONNIE AND CLYDE**—what a legendary life!

# OLYMPIC GAMES FOR EVERYBODY ...

With tearful eyes, excited smiles, and the pride of representing their own countries, thousands of athletes paraded during the opening ceremony of the **Olympic Games in Rio de Janeiro** in **2016.** However, one of the longest and most intense rounds of **applause** was given to a small group of **10 athletes**, coming from 4 different countries, united in the **TEAM OF REFUGEES.** They were athletes who had escaped wars (or came from areas where they had been persecuted or in danger), coming together **under the Olympic flag, as if finally coming home.** Their stories gave hope to about 60 million people in the same situation— because sport also delivers a lot of wonderful stories!

# ... AND FOR NOBODY

**The Olympic Games are indeed a peaceful occasion** that welcomes and unites the citizens of the whole **world**, but it hasn't always been like that!

Despite **PIERRE'S** good intentions to maintain the **Olympic Truce** even in modern times, the Games were canceled ... well ... **3 times.** Wars caused the cancellation, in particular the two **World Wars**. Not even the Olympic spirit managed to stop the fighting in those difficult and sad years (**1916, 1940,** and **1944**). A very different circumstance, although still a serious one, caused the Games to be postponed for the very first time in history: the 2020 Olympics in Tokyo were halted by the Covid-19 pandemic, that forced the organizers to put the event on hold. However, it wasn't canceled, because the love for sport won't stop before any challenge!

### BAREFOOT!

For decades, the Olympic athletes preferred to run either wearing shoes that had a very **thin sole** or even **barefoot**, exactly like what used to happen during the ancient Games (incredible!). The first shoes specifically designed to help athletes (and their poor feet) started to be used in **1928** in **Amsterdam**.

# WHAT ARE YOU WEARING?

### AND WHAT ABOUT THE OUTFITS OF THE FIRST FEMALE ATHLETES ALLOWED AT THE OLYMPIC GAMES IN PARIS IN 1900?

They had to play **tennis** and **golf** wearing ankle-length dresses, with long sleeves and high necks. It didn't go any better when in Stockholm in **1912**, women competed in the swimming competitions for the first time. They wore swimwear that didn't have sleeves, yet it was **long, all the way down to the thigh, and made of wool!**

# So cold!

The first **Olympic skiers** didn't wear comfortable gear either. They would ski **without a helmet**, either bare-faced or with a balaclava at most.

**Soooo cold ... and so painful when they fell!** They also wore uncomfortable **knickerbockers** (i.e., pants that were baggy around the thigh and really narrow below the knee) and **simple woollen sweaters,** sometimes even handmade. It was nothing compared to the ultra-light ski suits that are worn today! The life of the athletes has definitely improved, and perhaps the modern champions wouldn't be able to beat their Olympic "ancestors" if they had to wear those outfits.

**What do you think?**

# MYSTERIOUS OBJECTS

## HEAVY BALLS ...

Up until the **1950s**, soccer balls (even the ones used in the Olympic Games) were **sewn in an irregular way** and they would become very heavy when soaked.
**THE REASON?** The leather that was on the outside was not waterproof (which means that it absorbed water), so the ball would become very difficult to control.

Furthermore, just think how painful it must have been when players tried to hit it with their head!
The first **modern** balls were introduced in the **1970s** and were **black and white**: these colors were chosen because they were well visible on **TV** (at that time, TVs didn't have colorful images).

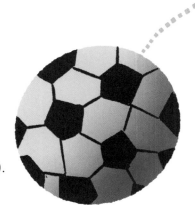

## ... AND HEAVY RACKETS!

Even **tennis** went through some small evolutions. For example, up until the late **1970s, rackets** were made of **wood**, they weighed about **14 ounces (400 g)**, and their strings were of animal origin. Today, the materials are all synthetic and they are slightly lighter (although several players say that a racket that is too light makes their strokes less powerful!).

## SO DANGEROUS!

Speaking of wood, even the first types of **skis** were rigid and bulky, and the boots wouldn't come off with a simple touch because they were actually attached to the skis.

THEY WERE DEFINITELY DANGEROUS AND NOT VERY PRACTICAL IN CASE OF ... A SUDDEN URGE TO GO TO THE BATHROOM (IT CAN HAPPEN IN THE COLD!).

# GREAT CHAMPIONS!

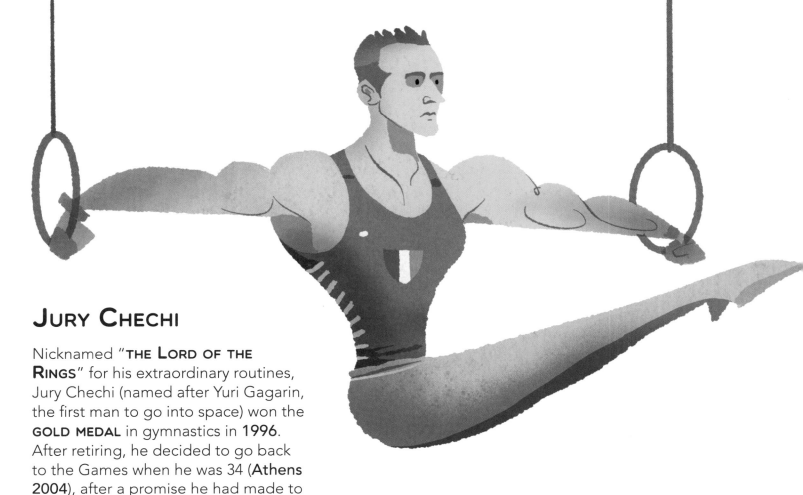

## JURY CHECHI

Nicknamed "**THE LORD OF THE RINGS**" for his extraordinary routines, Jury Chechi (named after Yuri Gagarin, the first man to go into space) won the **GOLD MEDAL** in gymnastics in **1996**. After retiring, he decided to go back to the Games when he was 34 (**Athens 2004**), after a promise he had made to his sick father. Mission impossible? Not for him—**HE WON THE BRONZE MEDAL!**

## FEDERICA PELLEGRINI

She started swimming even before she could walk and won a silver medal at the Games when only sixteen. Since then, Federica Pellegrini (known as "**THE DIVINE**") has continued winning and conquering the public's heart. Between **2007** and **2009**, she beat **9 WORLD RECORDS** . . .

## SIMONE BILES

Her grandparents raised her like their daughter, teaching her to believe in herself—a lesson that American Simone Biles put into practice at the Olympic Games in 2016, earning a **PLACE ON THE PODIUM 5 TIMES** (with **4 GOLD MEDALS**). That is how she has become the **gymnast with the highest number of medals in history.** Two flips have already been named after her (what an honor!).

## ZHANG YINING

During two unforgettable Games (**Athens 2004** and **Beijing 2008**), Zhang Yining's strength and precision allowed her to wrong-foot her opponents from all over the world and to win **4 GOLD MEDALS** in **table tennis** (also called ping pong), giving China and all her fans some incredible moments.
Aged 30, while still at her peak, she surprised the world again by announcing her retirement . . . to dedicate herself to **STUDYING**!

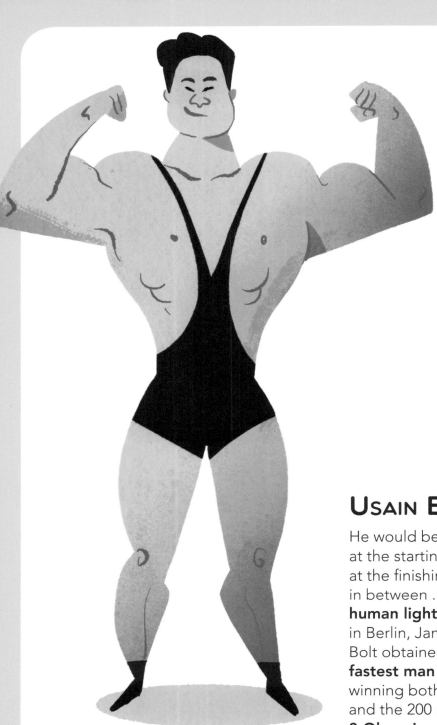

## Osamu Watanabe

The public at home was watching him, Japanese wrestler Osamu Watanabe, and he didn't disappoint them, as he won the **gold medal** in the **Olympic Games in Tokyo** in 1964. That medal was celebrated with great honors. It was his 186th **consecutive victory**, the last of many competitions where his opponents had never been able to score one single point (in any discipline!).

## Usain Bolt

He would behave cheekily at the starting blocks (and at the finishing line!) but in between ... **he was human lightning!** In 2009 in Berlin, Jamaican Usain Bolt obtained the record of **fastest man in the world**, winning both the 100 meters and the 200 meters. He won **8 Olympic gold medals** (between 2008 and 2016) and, most importantly, the support of the public.

He could really turn each race into a show!

# CHAMPIONS …
# OF FAIR PLAY

In 1963, the **PIERRE DE COUBERTIN** (yes, him again!) **MEDAL** was introduced, as an award to those Olympic athletes who might not have won a game but who performed generous acts that made them champions … of fair play (i.e., of **sportsmanship**).

Canadian sailor **LAWRENCE LEMIEUX** was one of the favorites at the Olympic Games of Seoul in 1988. During the race, the weather became terrible, with waves so high that it was almost impossible to see the orange buoys that were marking the path. Fortunately, he noticed something much more important: two athletes from another competition had fallen into the water because of the wind.

HE ABANDONED THE RACE TO RESCUE THEM AND HE ENDED UP IN 25TH POSITION, BUT WITH A SMILE. THIS IS TRUE OLYMPIC SPIRIT!

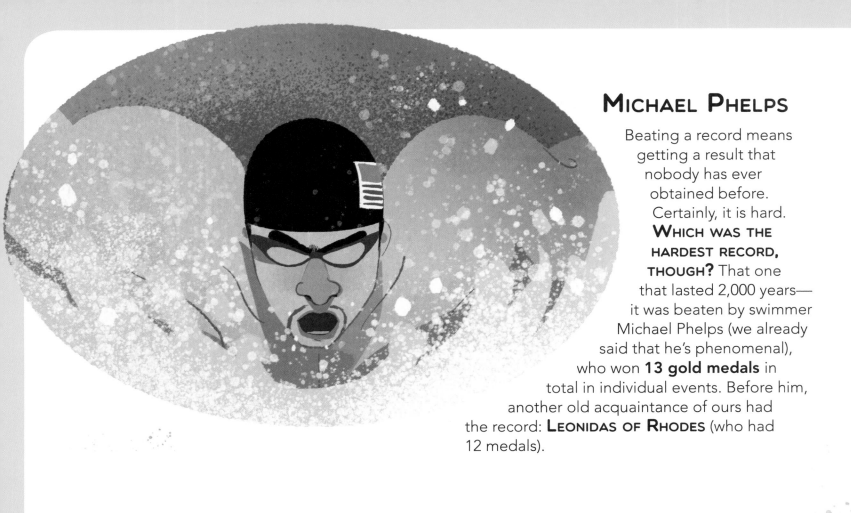

## MICHAEL PHELPS

Beating a record means getting a result that nobody has ever obtained before. Certainly, it is hard. **WHICH WAS THE HARDEST RECORD, THOUGH?** That one that lasted 2,000 years—it was beaten by swimmer Michael Phelps (we already said that he's phenomenal), who won **13 gold medals** in total in individual events. Before him, another old acquaintance of ours had the record: **LEONIDAS OF RHODES** (who had 12 medals).

# RECORD ATHLETES

## JOSEFA IDEM

Competing in the Olympics is the dream of every athlete, but doing it **8 times** seems to be an impossible achievement. Only very few have managed it, and only one **woman** is among them: Italian Josefa Idem, of German origin, who participated in the Games **from 1984 to 2012,** sailing the waters of the world aboard her **CANOE.**

## Nadia Comaneci

Being an **A+** student at school is difficult enough, but can you imagine at the Olympic Games? The Romanian gymnast Nadia Comaneci managed to become one in **Montréal** in 1976, when she was only **14**. It had never happened before and the judges struggled to post the score, because **the board would only reach 9.99**. In the end, they wrote only "1." They knew she was the best anyway!

## Carl Lewis

Can someone run so fast as to be named "**Son of the wind**"? Apparently, yes. Between 1984 and 1996, Carl Lewis earned this nickname by winning **10 medals** in 3 different running events (and he was a champion in the **long jump**, too!).

## Dick Fosbury

There was also someone who revolutionized an Olympic sport. In 1968, Dick Fosbury came up with a **new technique for the high jump**, which was rolling over the bar backward . . . and he won!

ALL ATHLETES HAVE BEEN JUMPING LIKE THIS EVER SINCE. IF THIS IS NOT A FIRST, WHAT IS?

# AGAINST ALL ADVERSITIES

## Im Dong-Hyun

In order to become a champion in **archery**, willpower and concentration are musts, but it is surprisingly not necessary to have perfect vision. **Don't you think so?** Well, Korean Im Dong-Hyun proved it! Even though he can hardly see from either eye (his nickname is "**The Blind Archer**"), he reached the Olympic podium **3 times** between 2004 and 2012.

## Alice Coachman

In **1948** in the USA, people of color didn't have the same rights as white people. And among all the unfair treatments, **they couldn't even access the athletic field**. That is why Alice Coachman, a champion in the high jump, trained in the endless green fields that **nature** provided! She got to the **Games in London** knowing that no black woman had ever won before.

**However, her willpower triumphed as she returned home with a gold medal around her neck.**

## Abebe Bikila

On September 10, 1960, Ethiopian Abebe Bikila won the gold medal for the **MARATHON IN ROME** after a 26-mile (42 km) run. All good, except for a detail that made his run become history—**he was barefoot**. He ran barefoot to honor his people, who were so poor that they couldn't even afford shoes.

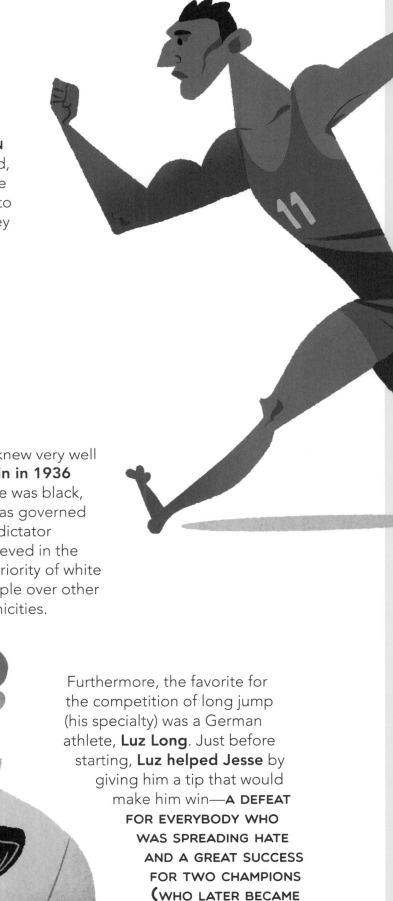

## Jesse Owens

USA athlete Jesse Owens knew very well that the **Games in Berlin in 1936** wouldn't be easy. He was black, and Germany was governed by **Hitler**, a dictator who believed in the superiority of white people over other ethnicities.

Furthermore, the favorite for the competition of long jump (his specialty) was a German athlete, **Luz Long**. Just before starting, **Luz helped Jesse** by giving him a tip that would make him win—**A DEFEAT FOR EVERYBODY WHO WAS SPREADING HATE AND A GREAT SUCCESS FOR TWO CHAMPIONS (WHO LATER BECAME FRIENDS).**

# THE WINTER OLYMPICS

THE IDEA DATED BACK TO **1897**: WHY NOT ORGANIZE ANOTHER OLYMPIC GAMES DEDICATED ENTIRELY TO WINTER SPORTS? HOWEVER, PIERRE WAS NOT SO SURE. AFTER ALL, NOT ALL COUNTRIES HAD A SUITABLE CLIMATE!

The fans of **snow** and **ice** had to wait until **1924** to have their INTERNATIONAL WEEK OF WINTER SPORTS (that's what it was called at the beginning).

Predictably, the attendance was poor: only **16 nations** participated with a total of **258 athletes** (very few, compared to the latest Olympic Games, where the total number reached almost 3,000).
Plus, it was so cold that **12 ATHLETES OUT OF 33** WITHDREW FROM THE CROSS-COUNTRY SKIING EVENT!

**WAS IT A COMPLETE DISASTER?** Not at all! It was an enormous success because everybody wanted to know about the quirks of the **6 disciplines** in the program (**biathlon, bobsleigh, curling, ice hockey, skiing, figure skating**). Such a contagious enthusiasm led the Olympic Committee to turn the event into an official Olympic Games. Up until **1992**, the Summer Games and the Winter Games were held in the same year (and in the same country) even though in different months. To give the audience even more enjoyment, **from 1994** it was decided to alternate the Summer and the Winter Games so there was an event every 2 years, with different host nations.

SINCE THEN, ON EACH EVEN YEAR, THE WHOLE WORLD HOLDS THEIR BREATH TO SEE THE PERFORMANCES OF CHAMPIONS OF EVERY SPORT ... AND IN EVERY CLIMATE!

For almost a century, the **Winter Olympics** have engaged athletes and audiences from every continent, even in those countries where it never snows, like **NIGERIA**, who in 2018 competed with an all-female team in **bobsleigh** (and you will find out that it wasn't the first time that this sport would bring a surprise).

**THE MANY DISCIPLINES PLAYED OUT ON SNOW AND ICE ARE SO ENTERTAINING!**

- **Biathlon**
- **Bobsleigh**
- **Nordic combined**
- **Curling**
- **Freestyle**

- **Ice hockey**
- **Figure skating**
- **Speed skating**
- **Ski jumping**
- **Alpine skiing**

- **Cross-country skiing**
- **Short track**
- **Skeleton**
- **Luge**
- **Snowboard**

SOME OF THESE DISCIPLINES WERE ALREADY FAMOUS, AND OTHERS HAVE BECOME SO THANKS TO THE OLYMPIC GAMES

**HAVE YOU EVER SEEN CURLING?**
The athletes slide special rounded **stones** (called "rocks") on the ice and push them using special **brooms.** Yes, that's what they are called!. Although it might look very easy, this sport is actually quite complex, as it consists of strategies and tactical maneuvers. It has been nicknamed "**ice chess.**"

# KINGS AND QUEENS OF WINTER

### CAROLINA KOSTNER

*"The most important thing that sport teaches you is to accept that you don't always win. It is not the end of the world if you fall, even in life."*

**DO YOU AGREE WITH THESE WORDS BY THE QUEEN OF ICE CAROLINA KOSTNER?** When she skates, she is as light and elegant as a dancer. However, she had to face some tough defeats and setbacks. But she got up . . . and won again, in life and in sport (including an Olympic bronze in 2014).

### STEVEN JOHN BRADBURY

In 2002, in Salt Lake City, Australian Steven John Bradbury won a gold medal, possibly the most unbelievable one ever. He was at the Games with very little hope: he had had a lot of misfortune in the previous 8 years and two serious accidents.

**HOWEVER, HE SURPRISINGLY GOT TO THE FINAL OF SHORT TRACK (SPEED SKATING) AND ALL HIS OPPONENTS FELL, ONE AFTER THE OTHER. YES, HE COULDN'T BELIEVE HE CROSSED THE FINISHING LINE AS A WINNER!**

## YUZURU HANYU

Imagine that you have to leave your favorite toy behind. **TERRIBLE, RIGHT?** That is what Japanese skater Yuzuru Hanyu must have thought when they forced him to leave his **lucky charm** (a teddy bear) at home in **South Korea** in 2018. His fans knew this, so they covered the ice with dozens of teddy bears before his performance. This gesture of affection may have helped Yuzuru to win his gold, the second one after his victory in Russia in 2014.

## PITA TAUFATOFUA

With a name that sounds like a tongue-twister, Pita Taufatofua was an extraordinary Olympic double-discipline champion, winning a gold in both a Summer (**taekwondo**) and a Winter (**cross-country skiing**) Games. He also became very famous after the **opening ceremony of the Olympic Games of Pyeongchang** in 2018. **THE REASON?** He carried the flag of his country (**Tonga**, an island in Polynesia) bare-chested, even though it was really cold and all the other athletes were wearing heavy coats and ski suits!

# STRANGE BUT TRUE ...
# TODAY!

## JOANA BOLLING

Joana Bolling couldn't contain her excitement: she would take part in the **Olympic Games in Rio** with her **handball** team. However, everybody in her family was sad because her father was very sick and needed a new kidney. As soon as Joana found out, she decided that the Olympic Games could wait. After a difficult operation (which luckily went very well), she donated a kidney to her father. **A TRUE CHAMPION, DON'T YOU THINK?**

## BOBSLEIGHING ... IN THE CARIBBEAN!

If you lived in the **Caribbean Islands** (where it's hot all year round), you could practice a lot of sports, but perhaps **bobsleigh** would be the last discipline to come to your mind. However, over 30 years ago, four fearless men from **Jamaica** (where there is no snow) started training for bobsleigh using ... **simple carts**. They managed to get to the **Olympic Games in Calgary in 1988**!

**THE COMPETITION TURNED OUT TO BE A DISASTER FOR THEM, BUT THEIR STORY WAS SO BEAUTIFUL THAT IT INSPIRED A MOVIE!**

## SHIZO KANAKURI

Marathon runner Shizo Kanakuri vanished during the **Games in Stockholm in 1912**. A true mystery—nobody could find him anywhere! Fifty years later, a journalist discovered the truth: during the race, because of the intense heat, he had stopped and had **fallen asleep**. HE WAS SO EMBARRASSED that he secretly went back to Japan.

HE WAS OFFICIALLY INVITED TO FINISH THE RACE, AND SO HE CREATED A VERY PERSONAL RECORD: **54** YEARS, **8** MONTHS, **6** DAYS, AND A HANDFUL OF HOURS. WELL, EVERYBODY IN THEIR OWN TIME!

## YUSRA MARDINI

The **rubber dinghy** was about to sink and the 20 people on board couldn't swim ... except for Yusra Mardini and her sister. Escaping the **war in Syria** through the **Aegean Sea**, they could not give up with the Greek coast only a few miles away! They jumped into the water, **dragged the dinghy** all the way to the coast, and saved everybody. TODAY, YUSRA IS A STAR IN THE SWIMMING WORLD AND COMPETED IN THE OLYMPIC GAMES IN **2016**, BRINGING HOPE TO MILLIONS OF PEOPLE.

Every 4 years, thousands of athletes (in 2016 in Rio, there were 4,350) take part in another world-famous sporting event: the Paralympics ("para" stands for "parallel," because they are organized along with the Olympics).

# NEVER GIVE UP:
# THE PARALYMPIC GAMES

We are still talking about fantastic champions, who break records and win medals. **So, what is so special about them?** Some of them **compete in wheelchairs**, others use **prosthetics** that make them look like superheroes, others **can't see or hear**, and others have a brain that functions in a **special way**.

**They are exceptional men and women who have managed to break through every limit (and every prejudice!).**

# HOW WERE THE PARALYMPICS CREATED?

In 1948, a doctor named **Ludwig Guttmann** (with similar ideas to Pierre's) decided to help the **wounded from the Second World War** by using **sport** as therapy. During the opening of the **Olympic Games in London,** he launched the **Stoke Mandeville Games**.

Only **16** athletes took part, but it was a good start nonetheless! The first edition of the **Paralympic Games** (in Rome in **1960**) saw **400 athletes from 23 countries** sharing the same infrastructures and equipment as all Olympic athletes.

IT WAS THE BEGINNING OF A PROFOUND REVOLUTION: NEW SPORTS—MORE AND MORE INCLUSIVE—AND NEW ATHLETES WITH WONDERFUL STORIES!

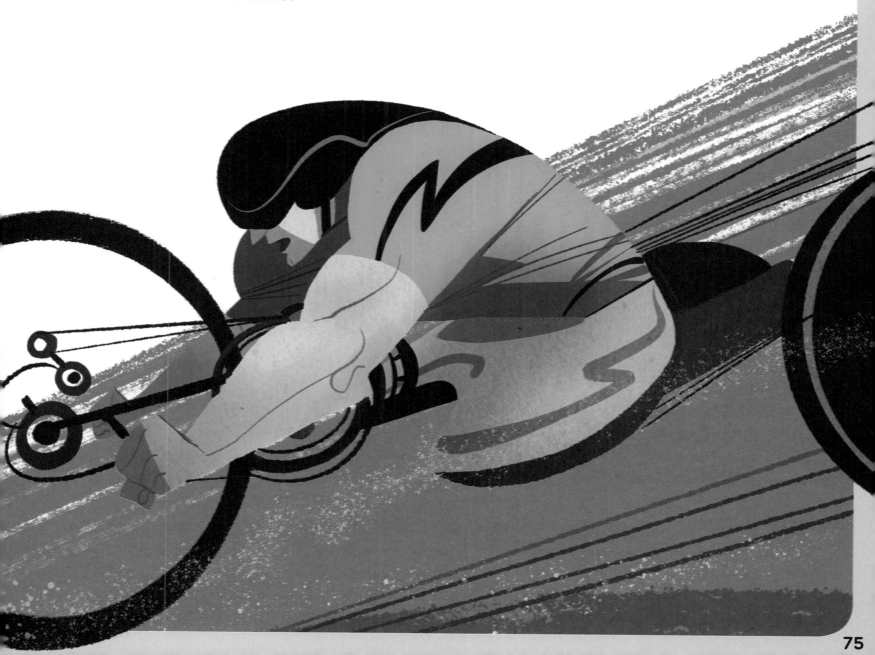

# THE CHAMPIONS

## ALEX ZANARDI

*"When I woke up, I was very happy because I was alive. That's how I am."* That is how Bologna-born Alex Zanardi describes the day that changed his life. On September, 15, **2001**, while **competing in a car race**, he had a horrific **accident** and **lost both his legs. WHAT COULD HE DO?** He had no doubt: he wanted to become one of the **most famous athletes in the world**!

## ABDELLATIF BAKA

He can't compete in the "traditional" Olympic Games because he's **visually impaired** (which means that he can't see as well as others), but if Algerian Abdellatif Baka had participated in the Games in **Rio** in **2016**, he would have won! That's right, because he is unbeatable in the **1500 meters!**

AT THE PARALYMPICS IN THE SAME YEAR, HIS TIME WAS BETTER THAN THAT OF THE RUNNER WHO WON THE GOLD MEDAL IN THE CORRESPONDING OLYMPIC DISCIPLINE.

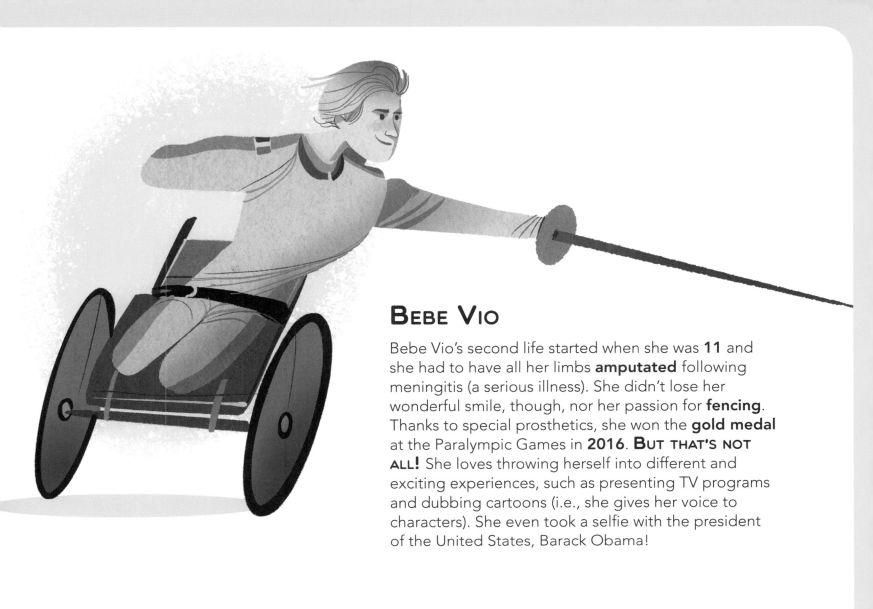

# BEBE VIO

Bebe Vio's second life started when she was **11** and she had to have all her limbs **amputated** following meningitis (a serious illness). She didn't lose her wonderful smile, though, nor her passion for **fencing**. Thanks to special prosthetics, she won the **gold medal** at the Paralympic Games in **2016**. **BUT THAT'S NOT ALL!** She loves throwing herself into different and exciting experiences, such as presenting TV programs and dubbing cartoons (i.e., she gives her voice to characters). She even took a selfie with the president of the United States, Barack Obama!

# TRISCHA ZORN

If she wore all the medals she won, Californian swimmer Trischa Zorn would probably double her weight (and she would have a real pain in her neck!). **Blind from birth**, she is the most successful athlete in the history of the Paralympics: she has won **55 medals** (of which **41 are gold**), after taking part in 7 Paralympic Games from 1980 to 2004.

# LOOKING FORWARD

**THE OLYMPIC GAMES ARE A GREAT ADVENTURE THAT WILL LEAD YOU TO TRAVEL TO EVERY PART OF THE WORLD. READY TO START?**

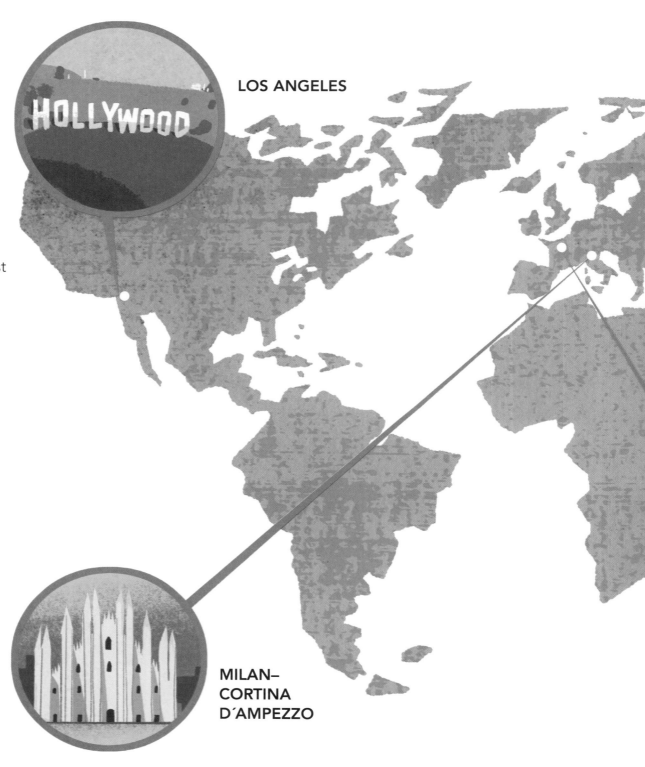

**LOS ANGELES**

**MILAN– CORTINA D´AMPEZZO**

## TOKYO 2020

The Games were announced with a colorful and exciting ceremony. Even the Japanese prime minister (one of the highest figures in the country) showed up dressed as a video game character! Although postponed because of the Covid-19 pandemic, these Games will always be known as Tokyo 2020.

## BEIJING 2022

In 2008, the Chinese capital hosted the Summer Games, which turned out to be the most expensive in history. Now, it's hosting the Winter Games, and China is aiming to break another record—that of sustainability (which means it is aiming to be the most attentive to the environment).

## PARIS 2024

The "City of Light" celebrates a very special centenary: a century will have passed since the last time it hosted the Games! It will be a unique experience, during which the French capital will turn into an enormous "Olympic field" to welcome not only athletes but also anyone who wants to discover its museums and monuments.

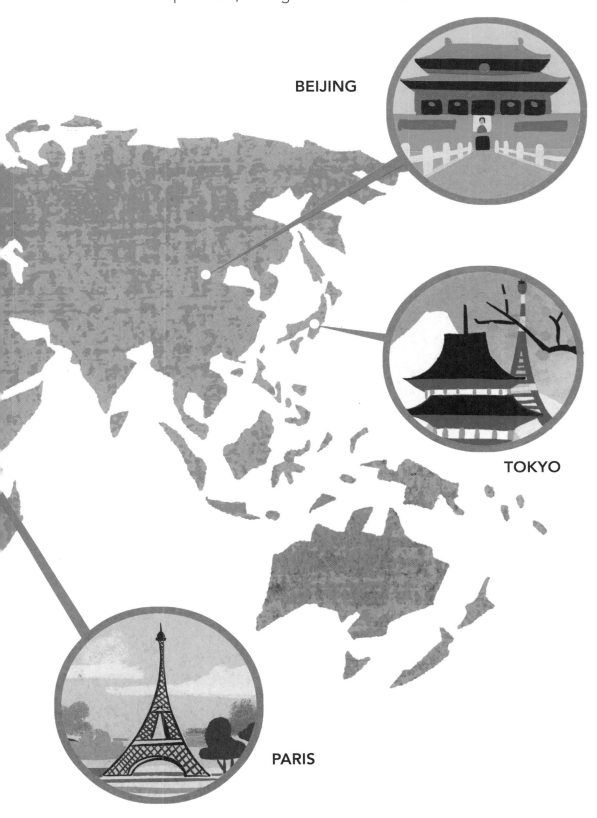

**BEIJING**

**TOKYO**

**PARIS**

## MILAN–CORTINA D'AMPEZZO 2026

The Games will split into two locations! Athletes and audiences will have to travel to the north of the country for the Games, in the midst of some truly breathtaking landscapes and towns. However, the closing ceremony will be held in a magical place: the ancient Roman amphitheater Arena of Verona.

## LOS ANGELES 2028

Creativity, optimism, diversity and inclusion. These are the values that Los Angeles wants to pass on during the Olympics, the same values that resonate with the authentic Olympic spirit. Along with the athletes, you will need to keep an eye out for movie stars!

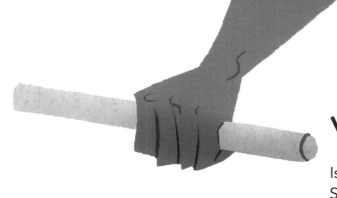

# VERUSKA MOTTA

Is a writer and author of children's books.
She has a strong passion for books,
comics, movies and television series.
She is a freelancer and communication
expert, and worked as a PR for an Italian
publishing house.

# LUCA POLI

He works with many of the most important
Italian children imprints.
Spacing from graphic design to illustrations,
he illustrated many books and worked with
several graphic design studios on animation and
adverstising. He never shies away from trying
new artistic styles and communication formats.
Every project is its own adventure . . . .
For White Star Kids he has illustrated "The Great
Book of Sports".

Graphic layout:

## VALENTINA FIGUS

**WSKids**
WHITE STAR KIDS
WS White Star Kids® is a registered trademark property
of White Star s.r.l.

© 2021 White Star s.r.l.
Piazzale Luigi Cadorna, 6
20123 Milan, Italy
www.whitestar.it

Translation: Inga Sempel
Editing: Abby Young

ISBN 978-88-544-1653-6
1 2 3 4 5 6   25 24 23 22 21

Printed in Poland